UNTOUCHED

LOIS THOMPSON HOLLAND

www.TrueVinePublishing.org

Untouched Gold
By Lois Thompson Holland

Published by True Vine Publishing Company
P.O. Box 22448
Nashville TN 37202
www.TrueVinePublishing.org

Copyright © 2021 by Lois Thompson Holland
ISBN: 978-1-7375934-5-4

All rights reserved. No part of this publication may be reproduced in any form without the prior written permission from the author. All scripture references taken from King James Version unless otherwise noted.

TABLE OF CONTENTS

Dedication 5
Acknowledgements 6

The Seventies

Sula 8
Cherish It 10
I Too Am a Poet 12
Quality Relationship 13
Friends 15
Special Friends 16
*Assignment 17

The Struggle

The Struggle 20
 *Assignment 21
Roots 22
Fear 23
This and That 24
*Assignment 25
I Wish I Knew 27

The Eighties

In Retrospect 29
*Assignment 30
Time for Everything 31
Why 32

The Nineties

Which Window? 34
Gems 35
Mirror 36
Plight of the Black Male 37
Invisible Prisons 38
State of Happiness 39

The 21st Century (Awareness)

I Am Tired, But… 42
I Am Human 43

Inner Beauty 44
It's A Spiritual Reality 45
Your Voice Speaks 46
Woman, You Are… 47
"Show Me Love" 49
*Assignment 50
We Can Breathe Again 51
I Am Enough 52
Young Black America—Young White America 53

Feeling Tender

Emotional Support 56
Incredible Weekend 57
Behold, My Love 59
Your Love, Exclusively 60
Your Man 61
*Assignment 62
Alone 63
She Sought But Found Not 64
Confusion 66
Pain 67
Listen 68
Train Your Child 69
Coping With Mountains 70
Keeping On 71
Keep No Records 72

Christ the Source

The Source 74
Ego 75
Destruction 76
Conceited 77
Anger 78
*Assignment 79
Smile On His Face 80

About the Author 82

This book is dedicated to my husband, Freddy, our children, Erin and Erik, family, friends, and parents who have encouraged me to put my inner thoughts in print. When I write poetry, I am free...much like a strong eagle soaring into a space exclusively hers.

ACKNOWLEDGEMENTS

My sincere thanks goes to:

Tina George, my church member, who introduced me to True Vine Publishing Company and the CEO, Timothy Bond, a gentleman who was always professional.

To Erin H. Bailey, my daughter, whose devoted and incredible ability to provide me with so many ideas and whose uncensored, constructed criticism, kept me grounded.

To my grands, Jameson and Jas who wanted to read my poetry and help me write.

To my husband, Fred, who had very few words to say, but asked me often "Sweetheart, how is your book coming along?"

To my son, Erik, who said, "That's great, Mom"

To my family and my friends, who encouraged me to pick up my pen and say what I wanted to say.

To Edger Scott and Azzie Jackson, (R.I.P) minister and church member, who encouraged and believed in me, and if they were still here, would be proud of me.

"THE SEVENTIES"

This is the seventies as I remember. The Watergate Scandal happened, the Equal Rights Amendment (ERA) was approved by Congress and the Antiwar Movement began. Racial inequality still existed so people were still fighting for social and political rights. Blacks were still struggling to adapt to transitioning from segregation to integration.

Cities were divided, violent race riots were still occurring, and the jails were filled with brown and black people. Healthy dialogue or meaningful confrontation between blacks and whites were not methods used to educate or learn about our differences or our struggles. Desegregation was still new. Racial tension was rampant, but the black community was resilient and had overcome a lot. They endured and are continuing to endure even now in the 21st century.

Black leaders marched for racial equality and encouraged others to strive for excellence. Many black men and women set the tone for generational growth by going to college to build and become empowered. Blacks were making progress and starting the next chapter in their walk. The struggle continues and the pages are still turning.

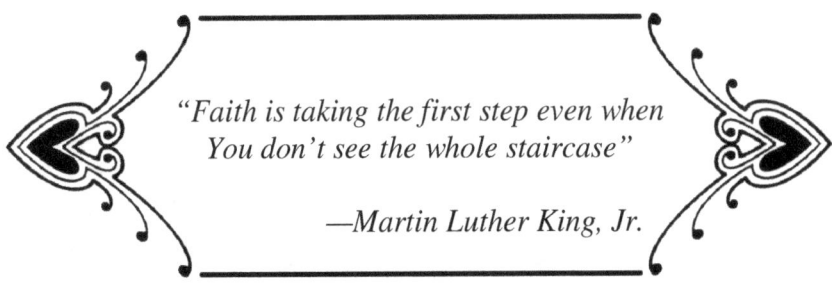

"Faith is taking the first step even when You don't see the whole staircase"

—Martin Luther King, Jr.

SULA

I once read
a book
called "Sula"
Sula was
a powerful
and strong
WOMAN
whose presence
permeated
a space,
an entire
town
she was
what icing
is to a
cake,
what butter is
to bread
even in
death,
her presence
awakened
an entire
town.
Sula
was
DYNAMITE!

Do you know a Sula? Write or Discuss.

CHERISH IT

What voices do I hear?

Once in a lifetime
Nelson Mandela, a Survivor
Martin L. King, a Fearless Leader
John F. Kennedy, an Advocate
Mahalia Jackson, a Melodious Gospel Singer
Marilyn Anderson, a Beautiful Soprano
Aretha Franklin, a R-E-S-P-E-C-T-ed Gem
Kenny G., a Harmonious Musician
Ray Charles, a Soulful Sound
Anita Baker, a Raptured Soul
Nikki Giovanni, an Empowering Poet
Toni Morrison, a Blunt Storyteller

My Mentors:
Edgar Scott, a Quiet Storm
Azzie Jackson, a Faithful Model
Jack Evans, a Dynamite Speaker

Family:
Mother, Shy but Powerful
Children, Sweet and Beloved
Sisters, Motherly and Accomplished
Brothers, Protectors, yet Wild

Cherish the bits and pieces in your life...
they are like puzzle pieces that create an image
for when they're gone
we only have the memories.

Who are your mentors and how have they impacted your journey? Write or Discuss.

I TOO AM A POET

I too
Am a poet
I pour my soul
out and
allow you
to
evade
my privacy
to open
doors that
otherwise
would be
locked and
labeled
"No Admittance"

QUALITY RELATIONSHIP

A good relationship
is like being
in a room
permeated and absorbed
with thoughts from
Nikki Giovanni
Toni Morrison
And
Maya Angelou
a good relationship
is like
Kenny G
making love
with his horn
and like
Anita Baker
as she becomes
totally
absorbed in the
lyrics that she sings
a good relationship
is like
Luther Vandross
singing
"Here and Now"
a good relationship
is like
sitting
at the feet of
Nelson Mandela
Edgar Scott

Azzie Jackson
And
Jack Evans
as he preaches
the Gospel.
Satisfaction indeed.

FRIENDS

Friends are like
strong trees
that offer
shade
in the
midst of the sun,
friends overlook
my faults,
they comfort me
in the
midst of the storm
Friends are
available
for me-
they listen
and are
sensitive to
my needs-
friends act freely
and allow me
to be
MYSELF.

SPECIAL FRIENDS

Special friends
are special
They are special
indeed
They share a
friendship
that is
sudden
and intense
Personalities
find relief
in the emotions
that
friends share
They make
each other
laugh
they share
a birthright
that is
common and
unique
friends are
special.

ASSIGNMENT:

We realize that friends loveth at all times in Proverbs 17:17 and in Proverbs 18:24 Jesus is a friend that sticketh closer than a brother.

Are there any other comparisons concerning this type of special friendship? Write or Discuss:

_____
_____
_____
_____
_____
_____
_____
_____
_____
_____
_____
_____
_____
_____
_____
_____
_____
_____
_____

"THE STRUGGLE"

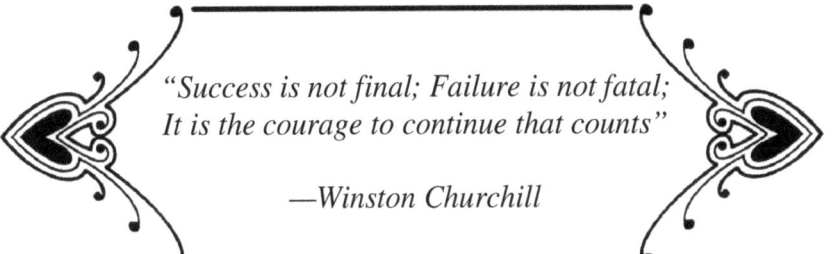

"Success is not final; Failure is not fatal;
It is the courage to continue that counts"

—Winston Churchill

THE STRUGGLE

Cool, groovy, jivey, bad
poverty, poor, comfortable, rich,
puny, strong, brave, hero,
mediocre, average, smart, brilliant,
lackadaisical, devoted, pious, religious,
unmotivated, creative, talented, ambitious,
unskilled, skilled, trained,
despair, agony, hope, faith,
shy, calm, soft-spoken, loud,
professional, entertainer, super-star,
and yet,
the struggle continues.

ASSIGNMENT:

After reading "The Struggle", think about the struggles that you have experienced. Reference the scripture 2 Corinthians 4:8-9 and reflect. Write or Discuss.

ROOTS

As I looked at Roots night after night
I went to work, and I wanted to fight.
They would say, "Hey, that isn't right
that happened a long time ago"
"Now you folks are on the go"
"On the go," I would say… "You just
don't know the struggle from day to
day." I am imprisoned by invisible
chains which make it hard for me to gain.
So let me be to think it out
I will be okay as long as
I SHOUT.

How did Roots make you feel? Then and now. Write or Discuss

_____
_____
_____
_____
_____
_____
_____
_____

FEAR

Fear, fear, fear
When did it begin?
Or can someone tell me
Where does it end?

Read and Discuss: Psalm 23:4; Psalm 34:9

THIS AND THAT

They say we lack this
they say we lack that
We began training
for this and that
and we still lack this and that.

ASSIGNMENT:

Do you find that "This and That" concept is still prevalent in 2021? Write or Discuss.

_____
_____
_____
_____
_____
_____

What is your THIS?

_____
_____
_____
_____
_____
_____

What is your THAT?

_____
_____
_____
_____
_____
_____

What are you doing about it?

I WISH I KNEW
(EJ#1)

I wish I knew how to be free
I'd fly like a bird
and nobody would capture me.
I wish I knew how to be free
I'd swim like a fish
from sea to sea.
I wish I knew how to be free
I'd loose these chains that
this capitalistic system
has used to bind me.
Oh--to be free—
I wish I knew how
it feels to be free.

Do you think that these capitalistic chains will ever cease? Write or Discuss.

_____
_____
_____
_____
_____
_____
_____

"THE EIGHTIES"

It's the eighties: The era of punk rock, big hair, and parachute pants. Rap music was birthed, and lyrics were flowing. Innovation and technology were emerging. It was a time of great pop culture, including new movies with Black leads and blockbuster like; "The Color Purple", "Do the Right Thing", "Purple Rain" and "Lean on Me". Music was heavily produced, and the sounds were evolving. Popular musicians emerged and created great music. Whitney Houston – "I Wanna Dance with Somebody", Lionel Richie "All Night Long", Michael Jackson – "Thriller", Madonna "Express Yourself", Billy Joel "Uptown Girl", Tina Turner – What's Love Got to Do with It? The tides were changing.

The hair was bigger, the world was younger, and everything seemed to operate on a different level of weirdness, but much remains the same. Racial disparities in the judicial system were still evident despite changing laws. Laws changes in the mid-20th century, but many people didn't.

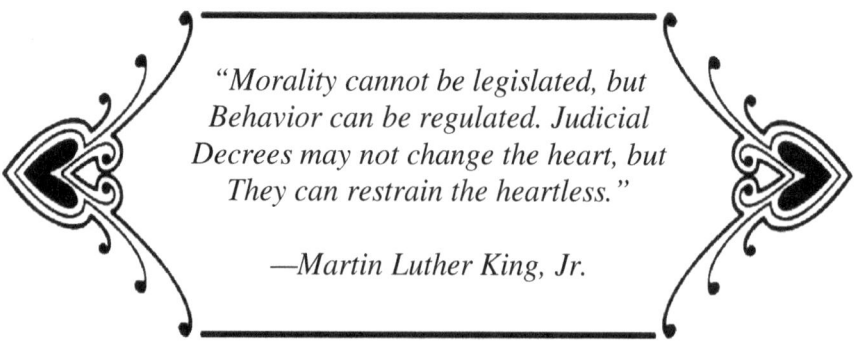

"Morality cannot be legislated, but Behavior can be regulated. Judicial Decrees may not change the heart, but They can restrain the heartless."

—Martin Luther King, Jr.

IN RETROSPECT

As I look
back
retrospectively
and
take inventory
of my life
I see
layers
of junk
peeled off
and
layers of
substance
put on.

ASSIGNMENT:

List your "Junk' and your "Substance". What would you change in retrospect? Write or Discuss.

List your Junk

List Your Substance

TIME FOR EVERYTHING

Brother-for everything
there is a season
and a time
for everything
under Heaven
a time to kill
a time to hate
a time to speak up
a time to rend
a time for war
and
a time to die
but make sure
God knows you.

Read Ecclesiastes 3 and "A Time for Everything". Write or Discuss.

_____
_____
_____
_____
_____
_____
_____
_____
_____

WHY

One man gives freely,
yet grows all the poorer

One man gives little,
yet grows all the richer

Fret not, my brother
each man will have his day!

"THE NINETIES"

A decade where the Gulf War emerged. Many eighties fashion trends were still popular. It was the era of DVDs, PlayStations, internet, and platform shoes, as well as embellished ensembles.

Janet Jackson, Lionel Richie, Prince and Michael Jackson were at the top of the Billboard charts. News stars like Mariah Carey and Toni Braxton were gaining status for their sounds and sexiness. It was a decade where pop culture took flight, new dance moves were born, and fast food was growing in popularity. Naomi Campbell and Tyra Banks were walking the catwalk. Bill Clinton became the 42nd President of the United States and some say he was the first Black President.

Blacks were gaining momentum. This was a decade of inspiration and empowerment, but the struggles were the same.

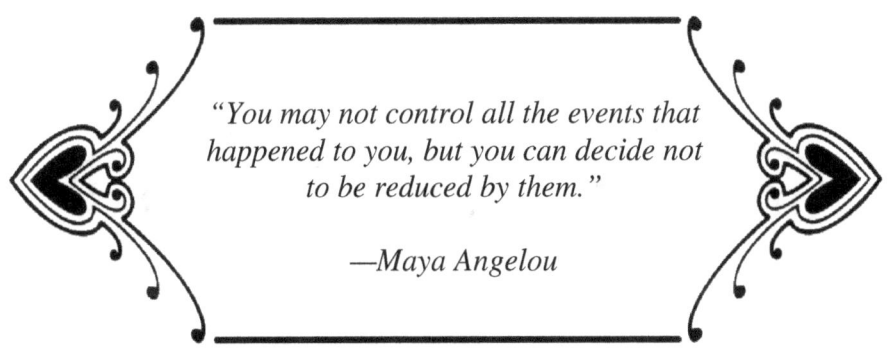

"You may not control all the events that happened to you, but you can decide not to be reduced by them."

—Maya Angelou

WHICH WINDOW?

Children must
learn
to decorate
their own
windows
Parents view
their world
through
windows of yesterday
and children view
their world
out of the
windows of now
Sometimes
this present
state of
"nowness"
lead to
heartaches
and
destruction.

GEMS
(For E.J. #1 and E.J. #2)

You are almost
knocking on
the door
of
adulthood
but
you are still
gems
precious diamonds
with brilliancy
that shines through
the door of
my heart.

MIRROR

Looking in
the mirror
I can see
layers of junk
that I must
look through doors
to unload
so that
I can
find out
whom I AM
and whose
I AM.

What kind of junk do you need to unload? Write or Discuss.

_____
_____
_____
_____
_____
_____
_____
_____
_____

PLIGHT OF THE BLACK MALE (#1)

The plight of black males
does not
always result
in his family life
Instead
the destruction
sometimes comes
from his perception
of life
and what
he expects
to get out of it
In his quest
for a
certain lifestyle
he gets
devastation
PAIN and imprisonment.

INVISIBLE PRISONS

Many of us in this
great big world
of ours
create invisible
prisons to
surround us
and often we become
immobile
and
paralyzed
to the point
of no return.

STATE OF HAPPINESS
(For Black Men Everywhere)

One day
if even in
my dream
I would
be in a state
of euphoria
if
I could drive
down the street
in any city
in any state
and
not see
Black men
drinking, wasting energy
and
valuable time
doing nothing
on the
corner

THE 21ST CENTURY "AWARENESS"

From the 1968 assassination of Martin Luther King, Jr. to the 2008 election of the first African American President, Barack H. Obama, to the widespread global protests declaring "Black Lives Matter", African American history in the United States has been filled with both strife and triumph.

Fifty years! That's how long I have been putting my thoughts on papers, throughout my journals and notes in my ledgers. It started in the seventies in Long Island, NY and has taken the journey with me not on in distance but also through many of my ups and down. Today, these poems have given me purpose, helped, and encouraged others and now, I am ready to share. Some of the notable milestones that took place from the end of the civil rights movement to the ongoing social and racial justice movements fueled my thoughts and took my emotions on a roller coaster ride. Today, I am encouraged, yet the journey was exhausting.

The hope was for change, but in 2021, we are still experiencing racism, both systemic and behavioral. The cry from black disillusioned boys and men are still as prevalent today as it was before. People are traumatized and angry, yet others are in denial and unaffected by what is going on. Systemic racism is getting recognized, police brutality is getting filmed, and inequality in the judicial system seems to be unchanged. We are progressing but nowhere near where we need to be. Fifty years of poetry and yet, the sentiment and themes of my thoughts are still relevant today. Black men are 2.5 times more likely to be killed by police and imprisoned 5.1 times higher. The prison system is over occupied with 56% of the United States incarcerated population being black or brown (NAACP). For some, these numbers are staggering; and to others, it is no surprise. Poverty, education, employment, and criminal history may be contributing factors, but aren't you tired?

> We are moving at a snail's pace and need to pick up the pace.
> We inch to progress but need to take leaps.
> We celebrate small wins but want to overcome.

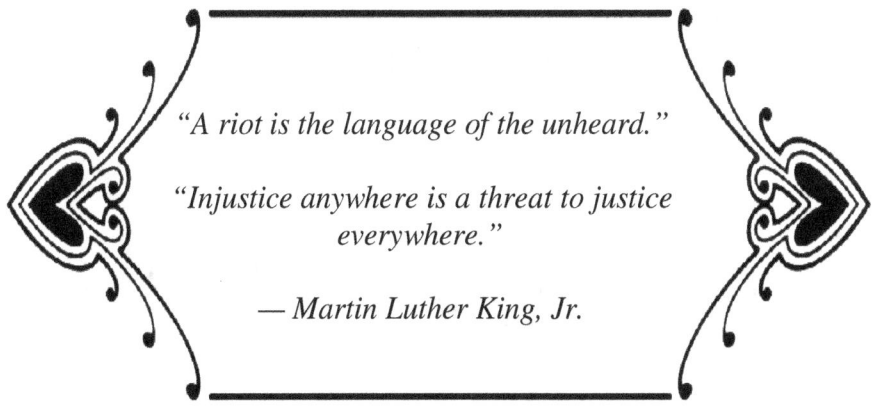

"A riot is the language of the unheard."

"Injustice anywhere is a threat to justice everywhere."

— *Martin Luther King, Jr.*

I AM TIRED, BUT...

I am tired, Oh yes, very tired
But I will not stop.
Nor will I give up.
My sons, my daughters and my family need me to stay around
Anyone "Black" needs me to make a sound.
I know along this journey, there will be hurt and pain,
For what happened to my ancestors, a permanent stain.
Yes, even though I am very tired...
My will is to stay around and protect them.
I will NOT give up.

I AM HUMAN

I am not
easily provoked
nor do I
fly into rage,
yield to
provocation,
become
embittered by
injuries,
or keep record
of wrongs,
but
I am
unseemly human.

INNER BEAUTY
(EJ#2)

There is inner beauty about a woman
who knows
whom she is and
whose she is.
She believes in herself
and knows
she can achieve anything she puts her mind to.
I see beauty in her determination
when she follows her own path and
can overcome any problem that she encounters.
I see beauty in a sister who has confidence in herself
and
can pick herself up when trouble comes.
She may fall but she can get up,
shake it off and move to the next level.

"IT'S A SPIRITUAL REALITY"

God has given Black culture a spiritual reality.
We have a gift that has been rubbed on us by God.
It was a gift that cannot be erased.
For us, it's a spiritual healing place.
It's a gift that keeps us going
Spiritual awareness that keeps flowing
When we want to give up on life
We turn to the one who made the ultimate sacrifice.

"YOUR VOICE SPEAKS..."

Your voice is Powerful.
Your voice is Edifying.
Your voice is Motivating.
Your voice is Empowering.
Your voice is Magic.
Your voice will Shape Someone.
Your voice gets a sister and a brother off their couch and believing in themselves
Keep using your VOICE so that they can expand and heal.
Your voice has Enlightened them.
Your voice speaks...

WOMAN, YOU ARE...

Spiritual Vessels that are

Brave, Strong, Intelligent, Sweet, Uplifting, Powerful, Adorable, Charming,
Delicate, Excellent, Inviting, Amazing, Super, Alluring, Adorable, Active,
Adventurous, Affectionate, Agreeable, Joyful, Kind-hearted, Kissable, Loyal,
Mature, Mesmerizing, Mischievous, Nurturing, Brilliant, Candid, Outgoing,
Religious, Patient, Photogenic, Confident, Considerate, and Creative.

Women stand on the shoulders of those who blazed the path before them.
You have no reason to stop and give up.
You are beyond description! You are all American.

Reflect on "Woman, You Are" and think about women that you know with these characteristics and how they have impacted your life. Write or Discuss.

_____
_____
_____
_____
_____

"SHOW ME LOVE"

Show me love so that I can be energized.
Show me love so that I can feel valued.
Show me love so that I can survive.
Show me love so that I can dream.
Show me love so that I can claim my roots.
Show me love so that I can be free.
If not, go your way, so that I can breathe and move forward!

ASSIGNMENT:

Read John 13:35; Proverbs 10:12 and Luke 6:27 and "Show Me Love".

Write or Discuss the comparison between "Show Me Love" and the above scriptures.

WE CAN BREATHE AGAIN

We are able to breathe
again because of the
verdict of the George Floyd trial.
It is a victory, but it took a while
Now we can smile.
Justice has been served
something we knew was deserved.
We shouted for joy when we heard the news
because Blacks have been so abused.
We have suffered for years
and have cried many tears.
For our fears.
For a few days, we can
breathe and Blacks will be pleased.

I AM ENOUGH

I am enough, YES, I am enough.
I am tough and stuff cannot call my bluff.
I have accomplished much by the grace of God
but I am not afraid
and you cannot intimidate me by your squad.
I am enough, YES, I am enough.
I am not frightened by the words
that you use and say about me,
because I am enlightened by my brightness.
No insecurities, no immaturity,
because I know that I AM ENOUGH!

YOUNG BLACK AMERICA – YOUNG WHITE AMERICA

I am an 80 year old African American woman with dignity
Who is inspired by your electric energy.

You have gotten up early and stayed late.
To protest against generations of hate.
Also to protest your disgust and hurt
Because of White folks' dirt.

Young White America
Your grandparents and parents are looking at your attitude
And how you are protesting with young Black America.
I am sure they are bit surprised as well as speechless
From which they once were preaching
And now wonder about their teaching.

I am so happy and encouraged by your commitment to change
And make the work better by your understanding to rearrange.
For now the world can be a better place
When discrimination can be erased.

Older folks like me wish that we could protest with you
And hold up the banner of solitude as you do.
But our aging legs do not permit
so we are proud to witness your grit.

So, I pledge my support before I die, I will continue to pray
And say "Thank You" for the energy that you display.

Thank you for giving me the hope to know
Your generation may change things before I go.
I salute you for your energy as people with passion and purpose.
Have I told you that you are Amazing?

FEELING TENDER

EMOTIONAL SUPPORT

Ask any
Woman
what she wants
from a
male
she will tell you
it ain't sex
it ain't the
movement of
his hands in
places where
she didn't
ask them to go
it is
emotional support.

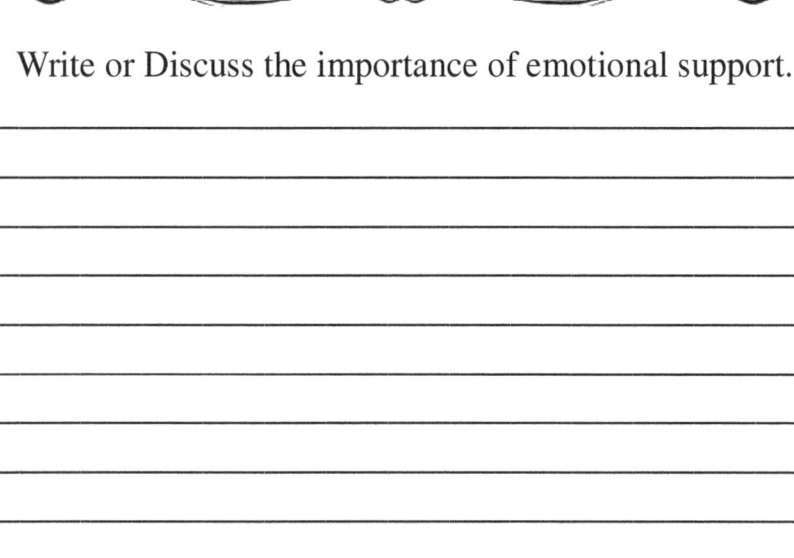

Write or Discuss the importance of emotional support.

_____
_____
_____
_____
_____
_____
_____
_____
_____
_____

INCREDIBLE WEEKEND

Come with
Me
for a weekend
of fantasy
One that will
permeate
your memory,
your soul
for endless ages
After I smear
melted chocolate
Over your body
to make it
smooth as porcelain
After my
chemistry works
with yours
and we disappear
into oneness
and experience
ecstasy
to the tenth power
If this fantasy
is not breathtaking
to you
I recommend separation
by way of death
because
you are void of
soul
and essence

What makes your weekend INCREDIBLE? Write or Discuss.

BEHOLD, MY LOVE
(With Special Love for Fred)

Behold, you are beautiful,
My love,
Behold, my love, you are distinguished
Among ten thousand
Your eyes are like spices
bathed in fine oils
Your teeth are like pearl
gathered from the sea
Your lips are like lilies
and your mouth is lovely
Your neck is strong
like the gazelle
yielding strength
Your hair is like
a flock of sheep
moving down the slope
of a steep mountain
Your body is like
works of ivory
encrusted with diamonds
You are all fair, my love
I see no flaw in you!

YOUR LOVE, EXCLUSIVELY

I want your love
Yet
you keep me on the bench
And I want
so desperately
to be back on your team
Tell me how
can I
activate
your emotions?
I need you
and want to
be fulfilled
by your love
Exclusive fulfillment is
all that I can accept
No more doggie bags
for me.

YOUR MAN

Sister, incline your ear
and hear the word of the wise
And apply your mind to knowledge
Love and cherish your man
Treat your man with care
Be faithful and loyal
and he will always be there.

ASSIGNMENT:

Read Corinthians 13:1-ff; Proverbs 17:17.a; and Romans 13:8.

Compare "Your Man" to the above scriptural references. Write or discuss your comparison.

ALONE

Night after night—
I sit alone
I think I wonder—
where my man has gone?
Will he come back
a week from today
or will he just stay away?
I cry, night after night
hoping that he will return
to take my sadness away.

SHE SOUGHT BUT FOUND NOT

Upon her bed by night
She sought him
whom her soul loves
She sought him
but found him not
She called him
but he gave no answer
She rises and go
about the streets
She sought him
but found him not
She called him
but he gave no answer
She returned to her bed by night
She sought him
but found him not
She called him
but he gave no answer.

Have you ever been rejected by someone you love? Write or Discuss.

_____
_____
_____
_____
_____

CONFUSION

A violent storm of confusion
beating gigantic waves of agony
crashed over my drained body
Suddenly, a monster of despair
tossed over me.
Death seemed
imminent.
In desperation, I searched the sky
hoping to see the comfort of
a cloud coming to protect me
from this vicious monster
that's out to swallow me.

PAIN

How can I
activate
your emotions?
My passport
was returned
and
you left me
standing
endlessly in
the line,
even though
I was
exhausted,
dazed and
glassy-eyed
You
forgot me.

LISTEN

Have you ever tried
to listen
to what I am
saying to you?
My words are
clear yet not
skilled in speech
nor eloquent
but the
message is
clear and one
that I have
been shouting for
30 years
are you deaf or
merely ignoring me?

TRAIN YOUR CHILD
(For Erik and Erin)

Train your child early
how to cope with problems
they will come everyday
the quicker they learn,
the faster they will
be on their way.

COPING WITH MOUNTAINS
(For Mother)

Learn how to climb mountains
She used to say
When you grow up—
They will get in your way
Mountains of oppression
Mountains of hatred
Mountains of fear
Mountains of depression
Mountains of ingratitude
Passed on to you
Mountains,
    Mountains,
        Mountains.
Don't forget to climb and climb high.

KEEPING ON
(For Dad)

DEPRESSED? YES!
OPPRESSED? YES!
HOPELESS? NO!
GIVEN UP? NO!
I Must Keep Pushing
In Spite of It all!

KEEP NO RECORDS

Keep no record about
what has happened to you
Otherwise, you can become defeated
and fail to reach that star
that's hovering over you
day and night
telling you
"To keep on keeping on!"

Compare "Keep No Records" to "Love" and I Corinthians. Write or Discuss your thoughts.

_____
_____
_____
_____
_____
_____
_____
_____
_____
_____
_____

CHRIST THE SOURCE

THE SOURCE

Christ came into
my life and
began to work
in me
He energized me
He rescued me
He elevated me
from the
abyss to the
mountaintop
I have been
redeemed by
His
Blood.

EGO

At midnight
I took
personal inventory
to see
what I could
do to get
closer to
God
The source
was there
all the time
but in my
struggle
for the
trivial
I
Edged
God
Out.

How do you **E**dge **G**od **O**ut? Write or Discuss.

_____
_____
_____
_____
_____
_____

DESTRUCTION

My streets are filled
with potholes
and my
drainage problem
is all backed up
I am tired of
living in
the cesspool
just as there is
a need for
a physical flushing
there is a need
for a
spiritual flushing
I found a light
and comforter
called
JESUS

CONCEITED
(For Lo)

You are conceited
because of your beauty
so they say...
If when I look
and see my beauty
don't blame me
for what I see…
My God made me!

ANGER
(For My Brothers)

Be not quick to anger
Anger lodges in the bosom of fools
Be not quick to anger
Anger drains all of your energy
Be not quick to anger
Anger is fierce
Be not quick to anger
Anger will force you to destroy others
Be not quick to anger
Anger robs you of true pleasures.

ASSIGNMENT:

In Ephesians 4:26 and Proverbs 15:1 anger is spoken of. Read both scriptures and based on your reaction to "Anger". Write or Discuss.

SMILE ON HIS FACE

I went to
a meeting
yesterday
with my
Christian
Sisters and Brothers,
I viewed their
inside index
and saw
disturbing characters
emerge,
I saw what
I thought was
new, put
on the old
and I saw
darts and
arrows
aimed toward
the heart.
It was
strange
because
I saw the
Devil
sitting nearby
with a smile
on his face.

If you want to change the world,
Pick up your pen and write.

ABOUT THE AUTHOR

Lois Raye Thompson Holland is well known from her obscure hometown of Bon Wier in East Texas, to the East of New York, to the snowy mountains of Colorado, to the beautiful cool climate of California, the windy city of Chicago and to the hot and humid, state of Texas.

To her husband and family, she is called, "Baby, and the Networker," to her church members, she is Sister Holland, and to her friends, she is known as 'Lois T'; Lady Lois T.H., "Diva" and to herself, she is "Lois Thompson Holland", "Lo Rae" a thoughtful sister, who is always energized, productive, and busy.

Lois began writing and reading poetry while living in New York in the seventies. She said that her "creative spirit" developed while listening to Nikki Giovanni and Maya Angelou. She would read poetry weekly to her students as a teacher of the auditory impaired at Lexington School for the Deaf. She often read work by Langston Hughes, Alex Haley, and Gwendolyn Brooks. When she moved back to Houston in the 1980's, she used to visit the Acres Homes Library, tucked in a corner to read poetry.

This book was birthed in the late 70's, and throughout each era of Lois' life, she wrote…and she wrote. This Poetry Book chronicles her journey over five decades and now, her book of poems, Untouched Gold, is finally going to print.

Lois is a graduate of Texas Southern University where she received her Bachelor and Masters Degrees. She received her certification from the University of Houston to teach the deaf and worked toward her doctorate degree at Columbia University in New York. Lois has written (3) three other books. **"Feeling Tender and Melancholy", "Bible Skits for All Ages", "Tips to Enhance Intimacy with Your Spouse"** and now, **"Untouched Gold"**

She resides in Houston, Texas, with her husband, Elder Freddy Holland of 57 ½ years. They have (2) adult children, Erik and Erin and (3) grandchildren, Ian, Jameson, and Jas. She retired in 2002 from Houston Independent School District and is living her best life making a difference.

www.ingramcontent.com/pod-product-compliance
Lightning Source LLC
Chambersburg PA
CBHW062147100526
44589CB00014B/1722